W9-BNU-897

THE ANGELS

GOD'S MESSENGERS
AND
OUR HELPERS

By REV. LAWRENCE G. LOVASIK, S.V.D.
Divine Word Missionary

CATHOLIC BOOK PUBLISHING CO.
NEW YORK, N. Y.

NIHIL OBSTAT: Daniel V. Flynn, J.C.D., *Censor Librorum*
IMPRIMATUR: ✝ James P. Mahoney, D.D., *Vicar General, Archdiocese of New York*

God Made The Angels

GOD made all things from nothing by His almighty power. He made the angels. Angels are spirits — they have no bodies. They have a mind and a will, for they can know and love God. God gave them great wisdom, power, and holiness. They are His messengers and servants.

The Good Angels Defeat The Bad Angels

BEFORE letting the angels join Him in heaven, God wanted to see if they would obey Him.

Lucifer, whose name means "the carrier of light," was proud of his power. He turned against God and said: "I will not serve!"

But Michael — whose name means "Who is like God?" — arose to fight for God. The good angels joined him and they cast into hell Lucifer and the bad angels who followed him. The bad angels are now called devils.

3

An Angel Sends Adam And Eve Out Of Paradise

GOD also made Adam and Eve. He gave them grace, which made them His dear children. But they disobeyed God and lost His Grace and the right to heaven.

God sent His angels to lead them out of paradise. The angel had in his hand a flaming sword, which was a sign that God is just and must punish sin.

But God promised to send them a Redeemer, who would save all people from their sins.

PEOPLE began to forget God, but Abraham did not. So God promised to make him the father of a great people from whom would come the Savior of the world.

One hot day three strangers came to Abraham's tent. He gave them food. Abraham had no children. One of the strangers told him that in a year his wife Sarah would have a son. Abraham knew then that God Himself had come to him with two angels.

GOD said to Abraham, "Offer Me your son Isaac as a sacrifice." Abraham was ready to obey God. He made an altar and put wood upon it. He then tied Isaac upon the wood.

Just as Abraham was about to strike his son with the knife, an angel touched his hand and said, "Abraham, do not kill your son. God knows now that you truly love Him.

Then the angel told Abraham that God would bless him and that from his family the Savior of the world would one day be born.

BECAUSE the king of Egypt would not free the children of Israel, God sent an angel to punish the land of Egypt. At midnight the Angel of Death passed through the land, killing all the first-born sons of the Egyptians and also the first-born of all animals.

The Angel of Death spared the Israelites when he saw the blood of the lamb which God had commanded them to sprinkle on the doorposts. This was the first Passover. **7**

An Angel Touches The Lips Of Isaiah

ISAIAH was one of the greatest prophets whom God sent to the people of Israel. He saw a throne upon which the Lord was sitting. Angels stood around the throne and sang, "Holy, holy, holy, Lord God of hosts, all the earth is full of His glory!"

The temple shook and Isaiah was afraid. One of the angels took a burning coal from the altar. With it he touched the lips of Isaiah and said, "Your sins shall be taken away."

Raphael Is A Guide For Young Tobiah

TOBIT sent his son, Tobiah, into a faraway country to collect a debt. God sent him the Angel Raphael to show him the way. On the journey a large fish leaped from the water after Tobiah. The angel told him to take the heart, gall, and liver of the fish to make a medicine.

When Tobiah returned home, the angel told him to put the medicine made from the fish on the eyes of his old father. At once his father was able to see. Then the angel said, "I am the Angel Raphael, one of the seven who stand before the Lord."

Raphael is the patron saint of the sick, of travelers, and of young people.

9

THE Jewish people was looking for the Redeemer. God sent an angel named Gabriel to Zechariah, a priest, who was burning incense in the temple. The angel said, "Do not be afraid, Zechariah, for your prayer has been heard. Your wife Elizabeth, shall bear a son and you shall call him John."

10

He shall be filled with the Holy Spirit, and he shall prepare for the Lord a perfect people."

Zechariah said to the angel, "How am I to know this? I am an old man, and my wife too is old."

The angel said, "I am Gabriel. I stand before God. I was sent to speak to you and bring you the good news. You will not be able to speak because you have not believed me."

Elizabeth gave birth to a son. Zechariah wrote down the words, "His name is John." At once he could speak again and he praised God. The child became St. John the Baptist who pointed to Jesus and said, "This is the Lamb of God Who takes away the sin of the world."

The Angel Gabriel Speaks To Mary

THE Angel Gabriel, sent from God, said to a young girl named Mary, "Hail, full of grace! The Lord is with you. Blessed are you among women."

Mary was surprised. The angel said, "Do not fear, Mary. You have found favor with God. You shall be the mother of a Son, and give him the name Jesus. He shall be great, and shall be called the Son of God."

Mary asked the angel, "How can this be?"

The angel said to her, "The Holy Spirit shall come upon you, and the Holy One to be born shall be called the Son of God."

Mary said, "I am the servant of the Lord. Let it be as you say." With that the angel left her. At that moment the Son of God became man and the Virgin Mary became the Mother of God.

The Second Person of the Blessed Trinity took to Himself a body and soul like ours. He came man and lived among us. This is called the Incarnation. Jesus is both God and Man.

The coming of the angel to Mary is called the Annunciation, because the angel announced the birth of Jesus.

The Angels Adore The Son Of God

SOON after the birth of John the Baptist, Joseph had a dream. He saw an angel standing beside him. The angel said, "Joseph, son of David, do not be afraid to take Mary as your wife. She shall be the mother of a Son by the Holy Spirit. You shall call Him Jesus, for He will save His people from their sins."

Mary and Joseph traveled to Bethlehem to place their names upon a list by order of the Emperor because they were of the family of David. Because there was no room for them in the town, they had to spend the night in a stable. There Jesus, the Savior of the world, was born.

Mary wrapped her little son in soft clothes and laid Him in a manger. As she and Joseph adored the Divine Infant, hundreds of angels came to adore with them, for this was the Son of God Who became man for the love of people. The angels praised God for His mercy to a sinful world.

In this way God became man. He came down to earth and was born of the Virgin Mary for love of us. Angels praise God for His mercy to us.

An Angel Appears
To The Shepherds

ON THAT night some shepherds were watching their sheep in a field near Bethlehem. A great light shone upon them, and they saw an angel of the Lord standing before them. They were filled with fear as they saw how glorious the angel was.

"Do not be afraid," said the angel, "for I am bringing you good news of great joy for all the people. Today in the city of David is born a Savior, Who is Christ the Lord. You will find an infant wrapped in swaddling clothes and lying in a manger."

Many angels appeared singing: "Glory to God in the high heavens, peace on earth to those on whom His favor rests."

The shepherds said, "Let us go over to Bethlehem and see what the Lord has made known to us." They hurried and found Mary and Joseph and the baby lying in the manger. They adored the Infant Jesus.

An Angel Appears To Joseph

GOD sent an angel to Joseph, who spoke to him in a dream, saying, "Get up, take the Child and His mother and flee to Egypt. Stay there till I tell you, for Herod will try to kill the little Child." At once Joseph rose up in the night, and took his wife and her Child, to Egypt.

Some time later the angel again spoke to Joseph in a dream, saying, "You may now take the Child back, for the king who wanted to kill Him is dead."

Then Joseph took his wife and the little Child Jesus, and began his journey back to Nazareth.

WHEN Jesus was thirty years old, He left Nazareth to begin His preaching. He first went to the desert. There the devil led Him in thought to Jerusalem to the top of a high tower and said to Him, "Now show the people that You are the Son of God by throwing Yourself down to the ground.

But Jesus said to him, "Away with you, Satan!"

Angels of God came to serve Jesus in the desert and gave Him the food that He needed."

An Angel Gives Water Power To Heal

IN Jerusalem there was a pool beside which were lying a great crowd of sick, blind and crippled people. At certain times an angel came down to stir the water and gave it the power to heal. The first person to go down into the pool after the water was stirred was cured.

A man who had been a cripple for forty years said to Jesus, "I have no one to put me into the pool when the water is stirred."

Jesus said to him, "Rise, take up your mat and walk!" The man rose and walked away.

Jesus Teaches About Angels

WHEN Jesus was teaching the people, they brought little children to Him that He might bless them. He said, "Let the children come to Me. The kingdom of God belongs to such as these. See that you do no harm to one of these little ones; for their angels in heaven always see the face of My Father in heaven."

Jesus laid His hands on them and blessed them.

An Angel Comes To Comfort Jesus

IN THE Garden of Olives Jesus fell down upon the ground and prayed, "My Father, if it is possible, let this cup pass by. Still let it be as You will have it, not as I." Large drops of sweat like blood, caused by His suffering, fell from His face. Three times He prayed. Then an angel came and gave Him comfort and strength.

O N Easter Sunday morning, Jesus rose from the dead by His own divine power, as He had promised. In this way He showed that He was the Son of God.

That morning some women went very early to the tomb of Jesus. They were bringing spices to put on His body, but they did not find the body of Jesus. They saw sitting at each end of the open tomb young men in white garments.

One of the angels said to them, "Do not be afraid. You are looking for Jesus of Nazareth, Who was crucified. He is not here; He is risen. Go, tell His disciples that He will see them in Galilee."

FORTY days after Easter, five hundred followers of Jesus met on a mountain. There Jesus showed Himself to them. After giving them His last commands, He blessed them, and then began to rise in the air until a cloud covered Him.

While the followers were looking up, they saw two men, like angels, standing by them. "Men of Galilee," they said, "why do you stand here looking up at the skies? This Jesus Who has been taken from you will return to earth, just as you saw Him go up into the heavens."

An Angel Frees Peter From Prison

KING Herod arrested Peter and cast him into prison. An angel of the Lord stood beside him, and a light shone in the prison. The angel woke him, saying, "Get up quickly."

The angel told Peter to put on his sandals and cloak and to follow him. They passed by the guards and went through the gate of the city, though the gate was locked.

Peter was surprised and said, "Now I know for certain that the Lord has sent His angel and rescued me from the power of Herod."

When Peter came to his friends, they said, "It is His angel."

Angels Will Come With Jesus At The Last Judgme

JESUS will return at the Last Judgment. He once said, "When the Son of Man shall come in His majesty, and all angels with Him, He will sit on the throne of His glory; and before Him will be gathered all the nations. The King will say to those on His right hand, 'Come, you have My Father's blessing.' To those on His left He will say, 'Out of My sight you condemned, into everlasting fire prepared for the devil.'"

Angels Around The Throne Of The Lamb Of God

IN HIS vision of heaven, St. John, the Apostle, saw many angels and men clothed in white robes, and with palms in their hands. They cried out with a loud voice, "Worthy is the Lamb that was slain to receive power and riches, wisdom and strength, honor and glory and praise!"

All the angels bowed before the throne and adored God, saying, "To the One seated on the throne, and to the Lamb, be praise and honor, glory and might, forever!"

THE good angels love us because they love God, Who wants them to love us and to help us. They protect us in soul and body. They keep us from sin and from all dangers. They pray for us and help us to do good deeds.

The good angels help us to fight against the temptations which the bad angels cause us. Bad angels try to lead us into sin and to make us lose our soul.

Saint Michael is the leader of the heavenly armies of angels. He is the mighty protector of the Church against all her enemies.

The Church prays:
"Saint Michael the Archangel,
defend us in battle.
Protect us against the wickedness of the devil.
O prince of the angels,
by the power of God,
cast into hell Satan
and all the evil spirits
who want to lead souls into hell."

You Have A Guardian Angel

GOD has given you an angel to be your faithful friend and to help you while you are on earth. This angel is God's messenger to tell you what God wants you to do. He will keep your soul from sin and will protect your body from harm. He is called your Guardian Angel because he guards you from evil.

Your Guardian Angel loves you because God loves you. He loves you because your soul is so precious that Jesus shed His Blood on the cross to save it.

Ask your Guardian Angel to help you to save your soul so that you may see God in heaven forever.

Pray to him in these words:

"Angel of God, my guardian dear,
Through whom God's love protects me here;
Ever this day be at my side,
To rule and guide.
                    Amen."

Love Your Guardian Angel As Your Friend

HONOR and love your Guardian Angel as your friend, for God has given him to you. Thank him and obey him when he tells you to do what is right and to stay away from what is evil.

Pray to your Guardian Angel each morning and night, and when you need his help.

Other Great Books for Children

FIRST MASS BOOK—Ideal Children's Mass Book with all the official Mass prayers. Colored illustrations of the Mass and the Life of Christ. Confession and Communion Prayers.　　Ask for No. 808

The STORY OF JESUS—By Father Lovasik, S.V.D. A large-format book with magnificent full colored pictures for young readers to enjoy and learn about the life of Jesus. Each story is told in simple and direct words.　　Ask for No. 535

CATHOLIC PICTURE BIBLE—By Rev. L. Lovasik, S.V.D. Thrilling, inspiring and educational for all ages. Over 110 Bible stories retold in simple words, and illustrated in full color.　　Ask for No. 435

LIVES OF THE SAINTS—New Revised Edition. Short life of a Saint and prayer for every day of the year. Over 50 illustrations. Ideal for daily meditation and private study.　　Ask for No. 870

PICTURE BOOK OF SAINTS—By Rev. L. Lovasik, S.V.D. Illustrated lives of the Saints in full color. It clearly depicts the lives of over 100 popular Saints in word and picture.　　Ask for No. 235

Saint Joseph CHILDREN'S MISSAL—This new beautiful Children's Missal, illustrated throughout in full color. Includes official Responses by the people. An ideal gift for First Holy Communion.
Ask for No. 806

St. Joseph FIRST CHILDREN'S BIBLE—By Father Lovasik, S.V.D. Over 50 of the best-loved stories of the Bible retold for children. Each story is written in clear and simple language and illustrated by an attractive and superbly inspiring illustration. A perfect book for introducing very young children to the Bible.　　Ask for No. 135

WHEREVER CATHOLIC BOOKS ARE SOLD

Index

God Made the Angels 2

The Good Angels Defeat
    the Bad Angels 3

An Angel Sends Adam and Eve out of
    Paradise 4

Abraham Welcomes God
    and Two Angels 5

The Angel Stops Abraham
    from Killing His Son 6

The Angel of Death
    Punishes the Egyptians 7

An Angel Touches the Lips
    of Isaiah 8

Raphael Is a Guide for
    Young Tobiah 9

The Angel Appears to Zechariah ... 10

The Angel Gabriel Speaks to Mary 12

The Angels Adore the Son of God ... 14

An Angel Appears to the Shepherds 16